# The Art of Stick Dressing

by

## NORMAN TULIP

ex/

I.S.B.N. 0 946928 31 2
© 1988

Edited by A. D. C. Hamilton

First published by Frank Graham

Published by BUTLER AND BUTLER of Rothbury
Butler Publishing, Cliffside, Rothbury, Northumberland NE65 7YG
PRINTED BY HOWE BROTHERS (GATESHEAD) LTD.

Syon House.
Brentford.
Middlesex.
(Telephone Isleworth 2353.

Most people, and certainly all countrymen,
know what a Shepherd's Stick looks like and
that its function is not only to provide a staff
to lean upon, but also to act as an aid in
handling sheep.

The art of stick dressing is not new.
In its more extreme form, often with metal
embellishments, it is found in the Pastoral
Staff carried by certain dignitaries of the
Church as a symbol of the pastoral office and
authority, certainly since the 5th century A.D.

Doubtless for centuries shepherds have
found occupation and satisfaction through the
long winter evenings in shaping and carving,
in wood and sheep's horn, their sticks. That
which started as a hobby has become a real
art and in my experience has had a special
flowering in the last 50 years, particularly
in the Border country.

The author of this book is a master of
the art of stick dressing and in making known
to others how to attain the special skills
which he has so successfully developed himself
performs a signal service.

I hope that the book may be widely read and
that the study may persuade many, and particularly
those who live in sheep rearing areas throughout
the world, to take an interest in, and to
encourage those who will practice the art.

*Northumberland*

# CONTENTS

# INTRODUCTION

I am always surprised to learn that there are whole areas of the British Isles where no one has any idea what you mean when you say that your hobby is stick dressing. In the following chapters I shall try to explain what this lovely old craft is all about. For generations the shepherds and farm workers living among the remote Cheviot Hills and also along the Borders between England and Scotland have spent their long winter evenings carving away at the heads of crooks or walking sticks. Sometimes they would be working on a ram's horn, other times it could be a hazel block.

During the summer it was a common practice for the shepherd to leave his hill and go down to the local blacksmith's shop. There he would use the blacksmith's tools and vice to "set" a number of horns. The word "set" means that the rough horn is heated and shaped into the approximate shape of crook's head or perhaps a plain walking stick handle. There is a very great deal of difference between the two.

If the shepherd lived too far from the village blacksmith he would then use heat of his own preference for the shaping of the horn and he had, of course, only a limited choice. Boiling water was widely used and even the dying embers of a peat fire, but by far the best horns were shaped by holding them over the top of the glass chimney of a paraffin lamp. The method was to heat about 1" at a time so as to make it pliable enough to allow it to be pressed into the required shape. In order to do this successfully the help of a good strong vice is of the greatest importance.

It was mainly during the summer that the stick dresser built up a supply of shaped horns to last him through the winter months. One has always to bear in mind that the shepherd would have no electricity in the days I am referring to. Shepherds are of necessity practical men, skilled with their hands. My father's old shepherd, a bachelor, did all his own knitting, was even able to knit his own gloves and in addition was a splendid cook.

During the time I have practised this hobby the heat I have always used has been methylated spirits. What is required is a low flame, a little larger than the flame from a candle. Over this flame the horn is gently heated about 1" at a time. Then pressure is applied with the aid of a strong vice and a number of small hard wood blocks. The idea being to "win" a little every time you heat it. Provided you do not overheat and scorch the horn, it is quite possible to reheat it several times until you are satisfied that the shape of the horn head is to your liking. One stick dresser is able to recognise another's work even years after the crook or walking stick has been made. There is always just that little bit of difference that is noticeable to another stick dresser.

# THE TOOLS

Over the years the tools have changed very little; a good strong vice is most important, two or three rasps some with a half round side, a number of finer files of different grades, again some to have a half round side, coarse saw, hacksaw, coping saw, a good strong pocket knife kept always very sharp, and two or three grades of emery cloth, which can be bought by the yard. A hand-brace and a number of steel bits up to ½", a joiner's clamp for the final shaping of the horn head and fine joiner's chisels to carve with complete the range.

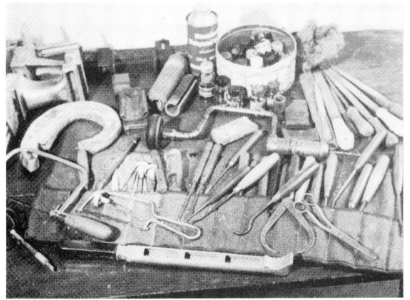

*Vice, saws, files, drills, chisels etc.*

To assist in shaping the horn after heating it is advisable to have a number of small hard wood blocks of various shapes. These are to use on the inside curve of the horn when in the vice jaws. It will also be necessary to have two or three pieces of curved iron about 3" long to protect the back of the horn when being pressed into shape in the vice. Another useful tool I have used to obtain maximum pressure is a small hydraulic jack welded into a special home-made framework.

For the very big horns it is advisable to have two strong steel plates about 12" square with a bolt hole in each corner, and when the whole horn is heated it can be placed between these two plates and flattened. The only electrical tool that I use is a small soldering iron for the feathering effect of the birds or the marking out of a trout's fins. It takes a great deal of courage to use a soldering iron on a horn, one is always aware of the fact you cannot rub these marks out, they are permanent and everyone can see them.

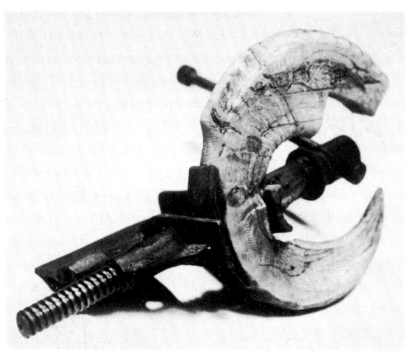

*Home made pressure clamp.*

The final rubbing down of the horn and the shank is done with steel wool, next the horn strapped with a damp cloth covered in Vim, and after all scratch marks are taken out the final polishing of the horn is done with Brasso.

## THE RAW MATERIALS

Today we are unable to obtain horns of anything like the quality that stick dressers were working with 50 years ago, the explanation for this being that the rams are not allowed to live so long. Today when the old rams have finished their working life they are sold for a worthwhile sum of money, whereas 50 years ago they would only be worth a few shillings, with the result that many were left on the hills to die a natural death. It is very difficult to find a supply of rams' horns, the best place to contact is an abatoir where these old rams are slaughtered, another source of supply could be the local hunt kennels or anyone who collects dead stock from the farms.

There is a very large spoilage of horns on the living ram. At an early age damage may be done to the horn through fighting which ruptures the blood vessels in the horn. Then there is the headfly that feeds at the base of the horn, with the result that the sheep will try to dislodge it by rubbing the horn against rocks or wire fences. It will also use its hind feet to get rid of the pest.

10

Inevitably some damage occurs to the horn and although it may be minor in the initial stages, frost and dirt may enter with increasingly harmful results as the rams grow older. Moreover, flockmasters often bore a coupling hole through the horn, and by tying two rams together it prevents them from straying.

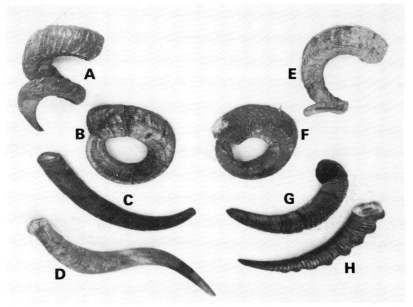

A *Swaledale ram.* B *Wiltshire horn ram.* C *Black buffalo.* D *Highland cow.* E *Blackface ram.* F *Dorset horn ram.* G *Jacobs sheep.* H *Cheviot goat.*

In the British Isles we have several breeds of horned sheep. Provided that the horn is from as old a ram as possible, it is possible to make a very worthwhile stick head from almost any of our native breeds. Some of the best horns I have ever had have been trophy heads from other countries. Having obtained a supply of horns it is best to allow the horns a period of seasoning, about one year is usually enough. It is almost impossible to get a "green" horn to keep its "set". By that I mean it is almost certain to twist ever so little back to its natural curve.

Shanks are most usually hazel, but blackthorn, apple, pear and indeed any wood of the right proportions. For myself I prefer holly cut larger than required and peeled and rasped to shape leaving the knots prominent.

The best time to cut shanks is when the tree is dormant and the sap is not flowing. But many old stick dressers say that the best time to cut a shank is when you first see it: otherwise someone else will have it.

## SHANKS

The wood most commonly used is Hazel. It is a waste of time to try and

11

straighten a shank when it is newly cut. Cut the straightest shanks that can be found and tie them firmly in bundles of about ten. Give the shanks at least a year to dry out. The bends can be taken out by using heat. For myself I use the same methylated spirit flame to heat the bends, taking great care not to damage the bark. If one is a little nervous about using a naked flame on the bark, it is possible to protect it by wrapping the shank in foil over the area to be heated. Having heated the bend the next step is to place the shank in a vice; this is where a length of rubber hosepipe comes in handy. Thread the shank through the hose and then secure it in the vice jaws. It is possible to straighten almost any shank by this method. It may be that a small percentage of shanks will rebel at this treatment. However, if your heat is right there should not be many disasters. Some stick dressers can successfully straighten a shank just by pulling it against their knee, after heating of course.

There is a wide difference in hazel shanks, most districts and counties have their own particular type of hazel tree. Some hazels are a good deal better than others. For instance, I always prefer a hazel that has grown among the rocks. The reason for this is that perhaps one gets a slower rate of growth resulting in a harder, tougher shank. Over the years one gathers quite a collection of shanks. It is at this point that one must guard against woodworm, especially if they are stored on the rafters in some old outhouse. Spraying the bundles of shanks before storage with a good, long life insecticide will deter woodworm attack. If you live in an area where cherry or blackthorn are available then by all means use these woods for the shanks. For many sticks I personally prefer holly. The shank is cut thicker than required for the final stick the bark is removed and it is then rasped and sandpapered to the desired dimensions. The method of straightening is exactly the same as that used for the hazel.

## BALANCE AND LENGTH OF SHANK

In stick dressing circles when we talk about balance we mean that the walking stick or crook is "clever" to handle. Great care should be taken in selecting the size and weight of shank to suit the size and weight of the horn. Failure to do so is a common fault, and many sticks are spoiled by forgetting this important point. The length of the shank is entirely up to the person who is going to use the stick. For instance, if one lives in the country and uses a stick a lot, the most popular length is about the breast height of the user. Whatever one does, always start with the shank longer than required because it is so easy to cut a little off at a time until the user has it to his or her liking. Another important point already mentioned is to try and proportion the horn head so that the nose of the head is never so long that it is below the join of the marriage to the shank. It looks far better when it is finished about ½" above the marriage. Proportion is one very important point that does not come easily to the beginner. I strongly advise any stick dresser to compete in the "Walking Stick" classes at agricultural shows. By doing this, it is possible to compare one's own work with other competitors. In this way it is sometimes very obvious to see where one is going wrong. Always pay particular attention to the show schedule because it is quite a common mistake for some competitors to enter his or her work in the wrong class with the result that the judge has no other option than to disqualify it.

## MARRIAGE OF THE HORN TO THE SHANK
### see Plain Horn Drawing Stage 2 page 16

One popular method is to drill a ½" diameter hole about 2" into the neck of the horn, then make a ½" dowel at the thick end of the hazel shank. The problem with this method is that it is extremely difficult to get the ½" hole and the dowel to agree with each other. Another method is take a 4" nail and insert the nail down the centre of the wood dowel. This is not too difficult to do because it is possible to follow the pith of the Hazel shank. However, whatever you do don't forget to saw off the nailhead. The reason for this is that should the Hazel shank ever get broken and it is necessary to have a new shank fitted, it is almost impossible to get the nail out of the horn if the nailhead has not been sawn off.

I personally do not favour either of these methods of marrying the horn to the shank. I prefer to use a 5/16" bolt about 5" long. The method is to drill a 5/16" hole about 2" into the horn and securely glue the bolt. This has several advantages. One is that you are able to grip the bolt stem in the jaws of the vice and with this method it is possible to carry out a fair amount of work on the horn head before it is fixed to the shank. It is also possible to bend the stem of the bolt so that the horn head is sitting true on the hazel shank. Should the shank ever get broken later on a new one is very easily fitted. With this method it is very important to finish off with the head standing like a sentry. Never fix the head so that it is drooping otherwise a stick looses all its character. A favourite trick of mine is to plumb the shank and the head against a door frame that is a few feet away. One gets very good sighting with this method. To put pressure on the marriage which is so necessary after gluing I always use a length of strong string. This string is wound round the horn just below the crown and then taken about 12" to 15" down the shank, securely fastened and then twisted to apply tension. At this stage the stick must be left until the glue is set hard. The neck of the horn should then be filed down to the exact diameter and shape of the shank taking great care not to damage the bark of the shank. One way to avoid this is to protect the shank with cellotape. NEVER use a coarse file for this final dressing down. The reason for this is quite simple. Some files make such a deep cut that it is almost impossible to finish the head without showing some of these file marks. So the golden rule is to stop in plenty of time. One can always take a little bit more off but one can never put it back. At this stage it is so very easy to become impatient.

The final fine shaping of the neck to the exact dimensions of the shank is done with emery cloth. The final polish of a plain horn is achieved with fine steel wool, Vim and Brasso in that order. The shank is finished in three coats of varnish, rubbing down between coats with very fine sandpaper. The best varnish for this purpose is a good yacht or boat varnish which has a high gloss, wears well and is waterproof. Fancy heads which are to be coloured should not be polished with Brasso, as this prevents the colour being evenly applied.

## THE PLAIN HORN WALKING STICK
### *see Drawings Stages 1 and 2. Pages 15 and 16.*

Anyone just starting to take up stick dressing as a hobby, should, I believe, start with the plain walking stick whether it is made from horn or from the one piece wood block.

There is ample opportunity to take up the fancy section of the craft later on. Selection of a suitable horn is the first step. The horn wants to have enough solid tip to make the hand piece from about 8″ if possible. For the plain stick the horn does not want to be too thick and bulky. The larger horns should be reserved for the fancy section.

Now every horn has a good side and a bad side. The bad side, by the way, is always against the ram's head. There are also no two horns alike even from the same sheep.

Every beginner I know is always surprised to find how much waste there is to cut away before reaching the solid portion of the horn. Having got rid of the waste, the next stage is to proportion the horn into three sections, always bearing in mind that the nose section does not want to be below the marriage of the handle to the shank. I always keep the nose tip about ½″ above the marriage, so if you have about 8″ to work with allow 3″ for the neck, about 3″ for the grip and the balance for the nose. Now comes the heating, and the use of the small chocks of hard wood and the curved pieces of iron that I mentioned earlier. Heat the horn about 1″ at a time and literally work your way round, steadily compressing it into the required shape. The 3″ for the neck wants to straighten up to the crown where the horn begins to curve for the hand (see diagram). It is from the CROWN that the head is balanced. Always avoid finishing the shape of the horn in such a way as to leave the nose end slightly drooping. In my opinion the whole head looses character if this is allowed to happen. After this first stage, it is now time to rasp the horn to the rough shape, always rasp the worst side first, but stop this rough rasping in plenty of time so that it is possible to take out the deep rasp cuts with a finer file. The horn should now be ready for the 5/16″ bolt to be fitted (see illustration). Drill a hole into the centre of the horn neck about 2″ in depth using a brace and bit and then glue the bolt in with a good glue leaving it until thoroughly set. The 4″ stem of the bolt that is later to go into the shank is of immense use for gripping the head in the vice. By being able to do this it saves any further damage to the horn when carrying out any other work. Now it is time to use the emery cloth. Never use a strip that is very wide, because there are some curves that have to be got round and if the strip is too wide it will "dig" in. After strapping with the emery cloth comes the time to select a suitable shank for the horn head. A fine type of head requires

14

a finer shank to balance the weight of the stick: likewise, a heavy head requires a heavier shank. The lighter type of walking stick may be ideally suited for a lady or a teenage girl, while the latter type would be more suitable for a man.

Having chosen a suitable shank, and again using brace and bit, drill a hole in the centre about 4" deep into the shank. Do not forget the escape hole for the surplus glue otherwise one will undoubtedly split the shank. The escape hole is just a very fine hole drilled from the side into the bottom of the hole in the shank. When the bolt is driven home with the glue into the hole the surplus glue can be expelled through this small escape hole.

## STAGE 1

## THE SHAPING OF A ROUGH HORN INTO A PLAIN WALKING STICK

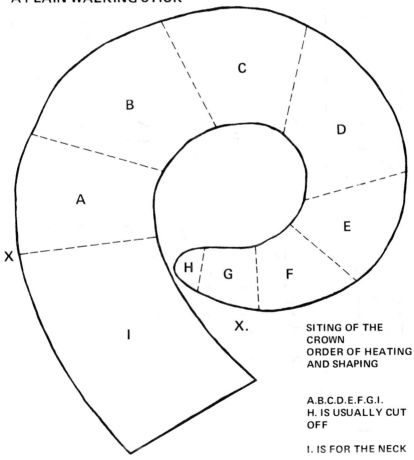

X. SITING OF THE CROWN
ORDER OF HEATING
AND SHAPING

A.B.C.D.E.F.G.I.
H. IS USUALLY CUT OFF

I. IS FOR THE NECK

# STAGE 2
## FINAL SHAPE OF A PLAIN HORN WALKING STICK

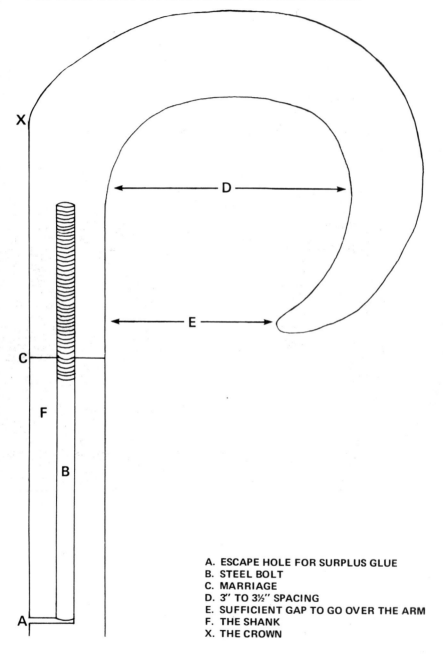

A. ESCAPE HOLE FOR SURPLUS GLUE
B. STEEL BOLT
C. MARRIAGE
D. 3" TO 3½" SPACING
E. SUFFICIENT GAP TO GO OVER THE ARM
F. THE SHANK
X. THE CROWN

**Plate 1. PLAIN STICKS**

*Left to right: Cheviot goat, Buffalo, Highland cow, Blackface ram, Chillingham wild cow, Ayrshire cow.*

17

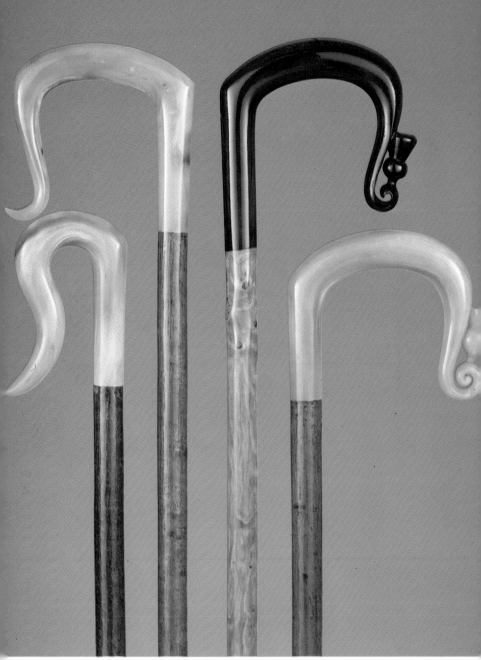

**Plate 2. WORKING CROOKS**

*Left to right: (a) Leg cleek. (b) Neck crook.*
*(c) Fancy buffalo neck crook. (d) Fancy ram horn crook.*

18

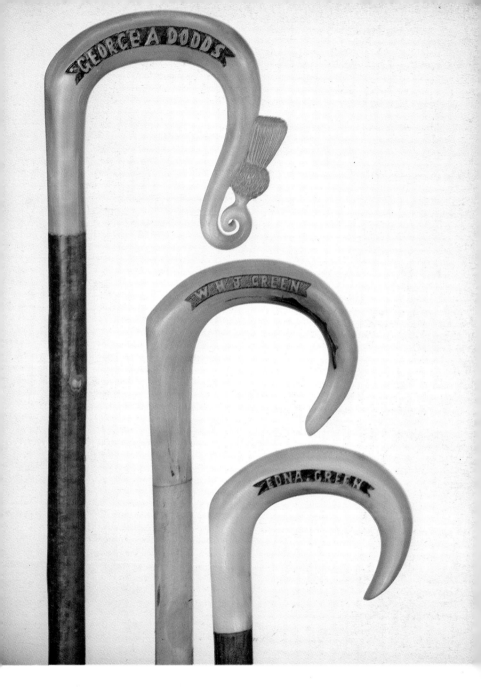

**Plate 3.**
*Left to right: (a) Fancy Crook. (b) and (c) Market sticks.*

19

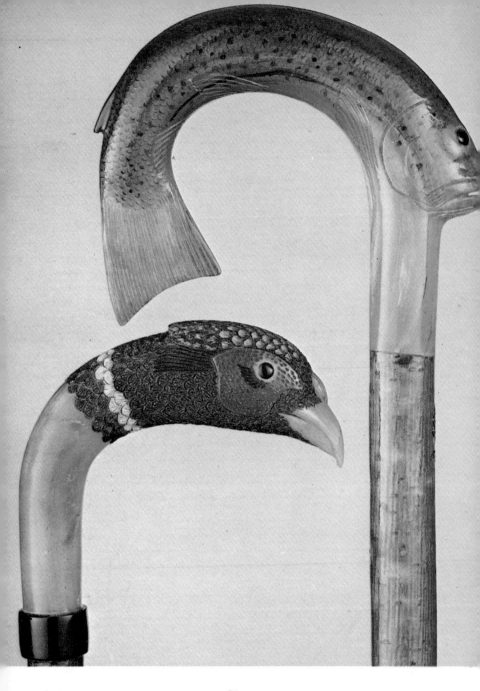

**Plate 4.**
*(a) Trout. (b) Pheasant's head.*

20

# COW HORN WALKING STICK
*Plate 1.*

It is possible to make a very lovely hand piece for a walking stick from a cow's horn. One would never realise that underneath the rough outside crust of a cow's horn there are so many exquisite colours. Like the ram's horn it is age that counts, the older the animal the better. A cow's horn is hollow like a water pipe except that it tapers to a point with very little solid at the point. Even the horn from one of Scotland's highland cattle will only have three or four inches of solid at the point. If it begins to bulk too quickly it is quite impossible to cope with this type of horn. The best horn to start with is possibly from an Ayrshire cow, it has length without too much width. After the bone core of the horn has been taken out it leaves quite a thin shell of horn, and at this stage it would appear to be quite useless to make any attempt to bend it. When a plumber bends a water pipe he uses a spiral to stop it from folding on itself. Exactly the same method has to be adopted in bending the cow's horn, only this time what is needed is a length of quickly grown sapling, such as a willow or rose briar. For myself I always prefer a rose briar and this is shaped to fit the core hole of the horn. The idea is to stop the thin shell of the horn from folding in on itself when shaping the head. An annoying fact about a cow's horn is that it does not curve one way. There are always two curves to contend with, and it is only after one tries to shape a horn that this fact becomes evident. Again the best type of heat for bending the horn is methylated spirits, always use a low flame no bigger than the flame from a candle. Unlike a ram's horn that can be heated several times, the cow's horn will not allow one to do this and if possible the correct shape has to be arrived at with one major heating. This is only possible if one visualises the finalised shape while in the rough horn. One should be very experienced in making a crook or walking stick from a ram's horn before ever trying cow horn and it is only after having a go that the difference between these two kinds of horn is fully appreciated. In short, one expects to finish up with a presentable stick when working with a ram's horn, whereas with a cow's horn the rate of success is very low. After all there are only about three men in Great Britain I know who can work successfully with cow's or buffalo's horn.

There are two ways of marrying the shank to the head. One is to take out the soft wood that is still inside the horn. Then reduce the shank to fit into the core hole so that it can be securely glued in. The other is to take out the soft wood then pack the core hole with horn filings mixed with glue and this is the method which I prefer. The marriage for this method is then the same as for the ram's horn. When filing a cow's or buffalo's horn into shape it is advisable never to use a coarse rasp. The reason for this is that some of the deep rasp marks are very difficult to take out and one has always to bear in mind that it is quite possible to file right through the shell of the horn, thereby making the horn useless. I have had this happen to me, but one learns the hard way. The final finish is to polish with steel wool, followed with Vim and finally with Brasso. It is just not possible to overdo this polishing with

Brasso. If you are going to exhibit sticks in competition get at them with Brasso the night before the competition. Never use varnish as it leaves a gummed up effect. Most judges do not like to handle and look at work that has been given several coats of varnish.

## THE PLAIN HORN WORKING CROOK
### *Plate 2 (b)*

For this particular stick the selection of a suitable horn is most important.

For instance, the horn must be about twice as long as the horn needed for the plain walking stick. The crook is made for a certain job and that is to catch a sheep by the neck. One must be able to pass four fingers between the nose and the neck of the horn head. The curve should be able to take the back of one's hand. If the size of the head is correct it is quite easy to keep control of a sheep. If, however, it is too big the sheep will twist itself free. Balance is most important. For instance, when the crook is being used by the shepherd it is being held by the wrong end, and if the crook is about 5 feet long it puts a great strain on the user's wrist. So the hazel shank should have hardly any taper. It is amazing how this can help the balance of the crook. There are several reasons for the shank of the crook being so long. If the shepherd is on a rough hillside it is of immense help to him in negotiating rough terrain. Also if one has a rough mountain gully to cross, it perhaps would be possible to hook onto a branch or root to seek assistance. Perhaps the most important reason would be to probe for sheep that have become buried during a snow storm. When a sheep is buried under snow it forms a tomb with its breath. The shepherd uses the long shank of the crook to probe through the depth of snow to find this tomb. Some of the shepherds are very experienced in being able to pin-point a buried sheep. What happens when a flock of sheep get buried is that they get driven by the force of the storm until they can go no further with the result that they lie down with exhaustion and eventually become buried.

During the winter of 1947 there were thousands of sheep lost in Northumberland in this manner. They were buried by such a depth of snow that it was impossible to find them. In fact, there were many hills where the entire flock was lost. It takes many years to breed the sheep back onto certain hills. The reason for this is that many hills have no fences, so the sheep have to become what we call "Hefted". By this I mean they are born onto a certain hill and both ewes and ewe lambs spend their entire life on this particular area of ground.

## THE LEG CLEEK
### *Plate 2 (a)*

This is a very practical stick and a great favourite with the border shepherds. When a shepherd is working at close quarters with a number of sheep it is so easy to reach into a packed number of sheep and draw out a single sheep with this stick. In fact once a flock of sheep are used to being caught by this method they will offer no resistance to a shepherd who is skilled with the use of the leg cleek. However, I must warn any beginner that it is only too easy to break a sheep's leg with this method. The cleek has to be exactly the right size so as not to allow the sheep to twist its leg after being caught; so one must stick to the old penny and the half-penny dimensions. Many of the dimensions concerning the size of various types of sticks and crooks that I quote are arrived at after years of use by the people who have had to have the assistance of a certain type of stick in order to help them with their daily work. It may be true that today they are perhaps used more for social occasions, such as county agricultural shows or some other such meeting; in fact, certain farmers I know would be completely lost without their stick; some of the older ones still have the same stick with their name carved into the horn that they have had all their lives. There is a particular farmer I have in mind and he will have had the same stick for about 70 years and it is still as good as the day it was made.

## MAKING THE LEG CLEEK

Selection of a suitable horn is of the utmost importance. The horn from a good Swaledale ram is perhaps the best; this is because the Swaledale horn is long and not too bulky at the head of the horn.

Straightening this particular type horn has many problems because as anyone with knowledge of it understands it curls two or even three times round.

As one heats and moulds the horn it is also straightened a little at a time; a buck rake prong is as good as anything to use as a lever. This can be a long and tedious process, leaving the horn nothing like the shape of a leg cleek. The horn will again need to be heated so as to bend it into the final shape. It is at this stage that it is necessary to proportion the horn out; so much for the neck, enough to go round the old one penny piece area and leaving enough for the nose: so put a chalk mark against each section. Finishing off is exactly the same as for the plain walking stick. The shank is usually not very long and should have no taper; the reason for this is that when the cleek is in use it is being held at the bottom end of the shank.

## THE ONE PIECE WOOD BLOCK CROOK AND WALKING STICK

The most favoured wood for this type of stick is from the hazel tree. When one is cutting shanks always be on the lookout for suitable material for the one piece stick. Sometimes a suitable shank and head will have to be dug out of the root below ground level. This can be very hard work and not very rewarding. The block that is likely to give the least trouble is the block that is obtained from a main stem. What one is on the lookout for is a good strong

23

shoot about the thickness of a 10p piece growing out of a main stem at a slight angle. The main stem wants to be thick enough to allow a suitable head to be carved out of it. Care should be taken in cutting it for it is very easy to split the block. Always cut well above and below what is wanted: it is so easy to trim off the surplus later on. Now it is most important to paint over with grease or paint the newly cut ends because, if this is not done, the block will undoubtedly crack and make it quite useless. The seasoning of the block may take two years or even longer. It is advisable not to hurry the seasoning in any way and to let nature take its course.

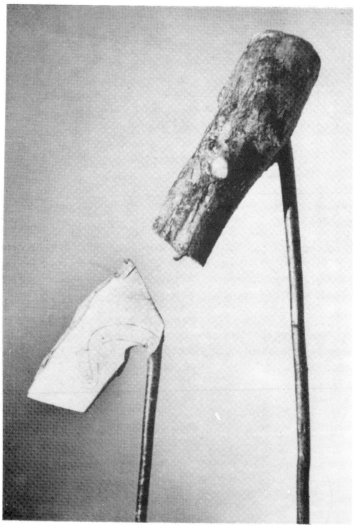

*As cut from hazel and sawn and marked to design.*

In making the one piece crook the first thing to do is to straighten out the shank. By doing this first it is possible to outline the crook or walking stick head properly to a greater degree of accuracy. The inside line is the most important. It is always possible to carve the outside line to suit the inside line. The final finishing of the head is quite difficult because the grain in the wood changes direction so many times. The making of this type of stick has never given me the same amount of pleasure as working with horn. As the block from which the head is going to be carved is round, it is helpful to have the two unwanted sides sawn off. However, a word of warning: always leave the centre part from which the head is going to be carved wider than is required. By doing this it is possible finally to true the head up by being able to move it just a little either way. Some stick dressers prefer to take the unwanted sides off, leaving the centre part with the nose end slightly wider than the crown end. By doing this it gives one a better chance of being able to curve the nose so that it is finished off looking right down the centre of the shank. The final finishing off of the head and the shank will have to be done with sandpaper and two or three coats of a good varnish. In my experience it is advisable to find a good varnish and stick to it, because two different brands of varnish sometimes will not mix.

## THE ORNAMENTAL OR FANCY CROOK
### Plate 3 (a)
This particular crook has stood the passage of time and is greatly favoured by Scotish crook makers. A common practice is to carve the owner's name into one side of the crook head and the name of the farm on the other. These would usually be carved with a small wood chisel or perhaps just with the shepherd's pocket knife. When carving the name, the most important thing to remember is that one has only a limited amount of space to get the letters into, so please experiment with the name before starting, because once you have made the first cut you are at the point of no return. It takes a great deal of courage to start cutting on a head that is already finished. The dimensions of an ornamental crook are exactly the same as for the plain crook, the only other important point being that one requires a slightly thicker nose from which to carve something else, such as a collie dog or a small trout. All I can say is don't be afraid to experiment. Mistakes are bound to be made, but this is how one learns. Always carve so that the carving is secure and will not have any part of it knocked off during use.

## THE PRACTICAL DECORATIVE STICK
### Plate 3 (b) and (c)
Many stick dressers like to make what I prefer to call the "market stick", to be carried on market day and at agricultural shows. Many farmers' sons are presented with this type of stick at a very early age. As it is about three-quarters of the size of the full crook it has ample space for the carving of the owner's name and place of residence. The scroll and thistle type is a

great favourite with many people. Others, especially shepherds, like to carve a collie dog that may have been a great favourite. Sometimes it would be carved in a sitting or a creeping position. It is very difficult to carve the creeping position because if you are not able to portray the alert movement of the collie when at work, the carving finishes up as a stiff figure with no character. There are many suitable subjects to carve on the nose of this type of stick. In many instances the owner's occupation or sport is the deciding factor. Of all the sticks that are made I firmly believe that this is the most popular and sought after stick of the lot, and will quite easily last anyone all their life even if they use it every day.

## THE FANCY SECTION OF STICK DRESSING

### THE MAKING OF A TROUT
*Plage 4 (a)*

In order to increase one's interest in stick dressing, I strongly advise everyone to have a go at the fancy section of the craft. A very good head is the brown trout. But before you start, obtain a trout because all our rivers have their own particular types. The selection of a suitable horn for this kind of head is of the utmost importance. One requires a broader, fuller horn with a fair

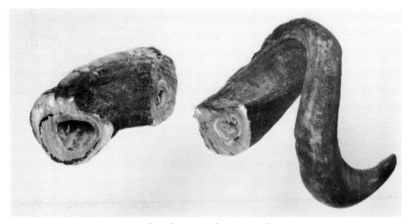

*Raw horn, surplus removed.*

amount of width for the tail. For instance, the trout's jaws are going to protrude if possible ½″ to ¾″ from the neck of the horn.

The body of the trout is literally moulded with the aid of the small blocks and pieces of curved iron that I have mentioned earlier. About 1″ of the horn is heated at a time until the trout's body is moulded into the curved poise of a leaping fish. After one is satisfied with the shape of the trout it is time to fix a bolt 1½″ to 2″ into the neck of the horn. By fixing the bolt at this stage one is able to grip the stem of the bolt in a vice while carrying out the rest of

26

# 9" RIVER TROUT OUTLINED IN A ROUGH HORN

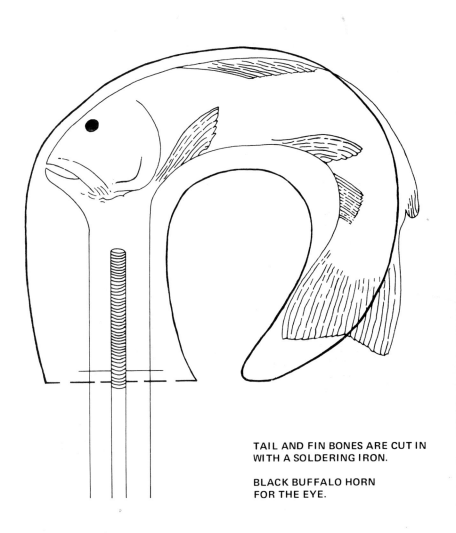

TAIL AND FIN BONES ARE CUT IN
WITH A SOLDERING IRON.

BLACK BUFFALO HORN
FOR THE EYE.

*Horn marked for cutting.*

the work. This is of great help for the simple reason that if you grip the body of the trout in the vice, it will receive marks that can never be taken out. Every horn has a good and a bad side and beginners are often bewildered and disheartened at the difference between the two sides. I always do the worst side first taking as little as possible away with the file. It is a fairly easy job to make the good side match the poorer one.

It is now vital that you should have obtained a 9" or 10" trout because one needs the exact measurements to a 1/16 of an inch from the nose to the eye then onto the gills down the body to the fins and finally to the tail. The colour also has to be noted and then the spots. Pay particular attention to these spots especially the red ones because they are not just thrown on any old how. It is really shattering to realise how little the average person knows about the trout. For instance, if the eye is in the right place the whole thing seems to come to life. The mouth also needs to have that rather surly expression that a trout's mouth has. It is the expression of the trout's head that is so hard to capture. The eye is made from black buffalo horn. By now the body will be fairly well filed down to shape, so it is time for the emery cloth. To do this take a 1" wide strip of fairly fine emery cloth and literally strap the trout all over until there are no file marks left. Now comes the time to draw the mouth, the eye and the gills, etc. A felt-nibbed pen is best for this. As I am right handed, I always draw the left side first for the simple reason that I can centre my pen so much more accurately by this method. A left handed person may prefer to do the right side first. The holes for the eyes want to be drilled between ¼" and ½" into the horn and into these holes is glued a round portion of the buffalo horn. What a hard job it is to get the two eyes alike! After marking out the mouth it requires to be finely cut in a slightly open position. A coping saw will do this quite easily. To clear away the saw marks inside the mouth a sharp pocket knife is required. For the cutting out of the gills and fins, including the bone structure of the tail, a set of fine joiner's wood carving chisels can be used or what I now prefer, a fine bitted electric soldering iron. This is where courage comes into the game because any mistakes now are there for all time and for everyone to see. So try to have your carving hand anchored and use the chisel slowly. The trout has now gone as far as it can and the next stage is to marry the almost finished head to the hazel shank. Drill a hole down the centre of the shank so that it is deep enough to take the 3" part of the bolt that has been used in the vice. The jaws of the vice will have roughed up the bolt stem so that the glue will stick to it. A bolt has the major advantage that it can be given a slight bend to assist in getting the head into this sentry-like stance. Never forget the inside line of any stick is the important one to look at in fixing the head. Give the bolt's stem a smearing of glue and then insert it into the hole that has

*Cut to rough shape.*

*Bolt fitted and tail shaped.*

been drilled into the shank. Work the bolt stem quietly down into the hole so that the surplus glue will be given time to escape. Now to apply the necessary pressure take a length of string, double it and tie it securely around the neck of the born. Let the two loose ends hang down the shank to about 12″ below the marriage. Securely tie the loose ends of the string around the hazel shank in such a way that they cannot slip up the shank. Then take a short pencil or whatever is handy and twist the string tight, leaving it like this until the glue is securely set. Also it gives the shank and the horn a period that one or even both will "crine" down just enough to leave a little step where the marriage takes place. After this the next stage is to carefully file the rough neck of the

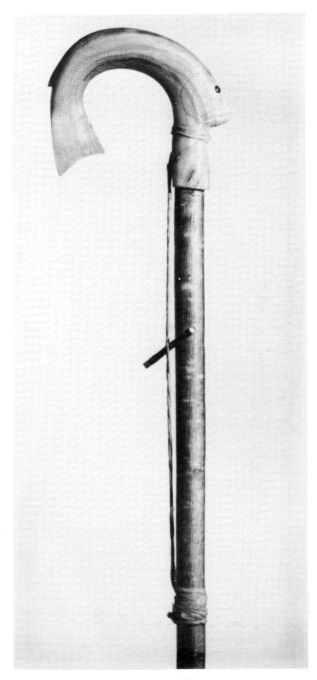

*Glueing to shank.*

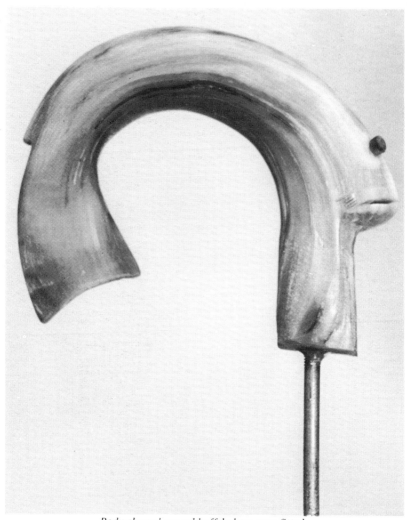

*Body cleaned up and buffalo horn eyes fitted.*

horn down to the size of the shank. In order to protect the bark from file damage it is always advisable to cellotape 2″ or 3″ from the marriage down the shank. This should give sufficient protection for this final finishing and polishing of the horn. We left the trout at a stage where it had been strapped with emery cloth and fins, etc., cut into the trout's body. The scales are marked by a circular punch. Emery cloth leaves marks which have to be polished away until not the slightest sign of a scratch is left. This is accomplished by polishing with fine steel wool. Make sure the steel wool is new and clean. After this comes the Vim. It is just not possible to overdo the polishing with Vim. Slightly dampen a cloth soaked with Vim, and simply get "stuck in".

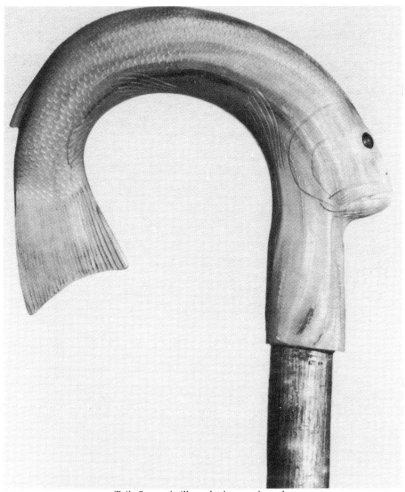

*Tail, fins and gill marked, eyes shaped.*

## THE COLOURING OF THE TROUT WITH INK

As I mentioned at the beginning, it is important to have a trout to study. Every river appears to have its own particular type and colour of fish. Even in Northumberland the difference is most noticeable, for although the River Aln is only three miles from the Coquet where it enters the sea, the trout from these two rivers are quite different in colour. The River Aln trout is a very much darker fish.

Ink is obtainable in many shades so that it is possible to match almost any colour. What you can also do is to mix them in order to tone down a colour. I do not advise the use of paint at any time. It is by no means easy to colour a

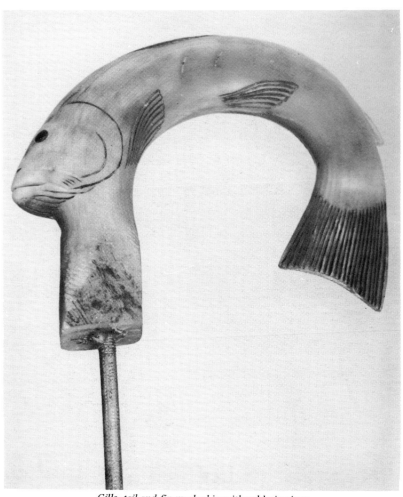

*Gills, tail and fin marked in with soldering iron.*

trout because the body of the trout has been polished to a glass-like finish making it rather difficult to absorb colour. So the golden rule is to apply only one coat of ink at a time and then let it dry. Should one make a mess of the colour the only thing to do is strip it all off with a damp cloth soaked with Vim or, in other words, start all over again. Quite a lot of stick dressers are cautious about using colour. Take particular notice of the position and numbers of the red spots, each side of the trout. There is a very definite pattern for the spots, so in order to avoid some fisherman criticising one's work, be careful about detail. After the use of colour it has to be sealed in with varnish. A good yacht varnish should be used for the very reason that cheap varnishes tend to become "tacky" in one's hand when using the stick for walking. The Hazel shank will also require two or three coats of the same varnish. Try if possible to use one brand of clear varnish because it often happens that a "fight" takes place between varnishes that are made by different firms.

To make a trout, cut the fins, etc., and to scale the body of the trout, colour and finish good enough to win a show would take me about 100 hours.

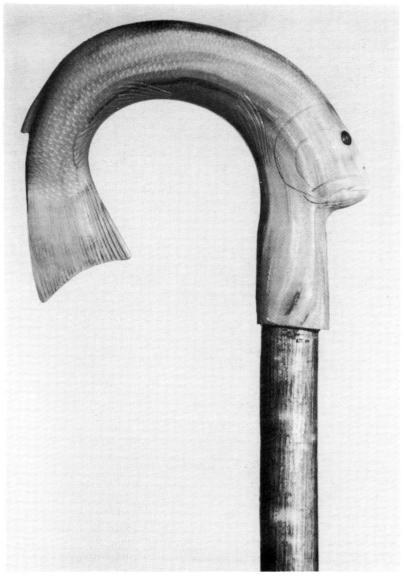

*Shanked and ready for filing to diameter of shank.*

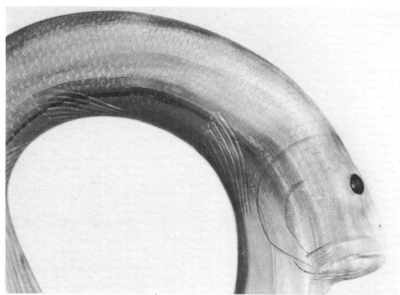

*After polishing and ready for colouring.*

*Coloured and varnished.*

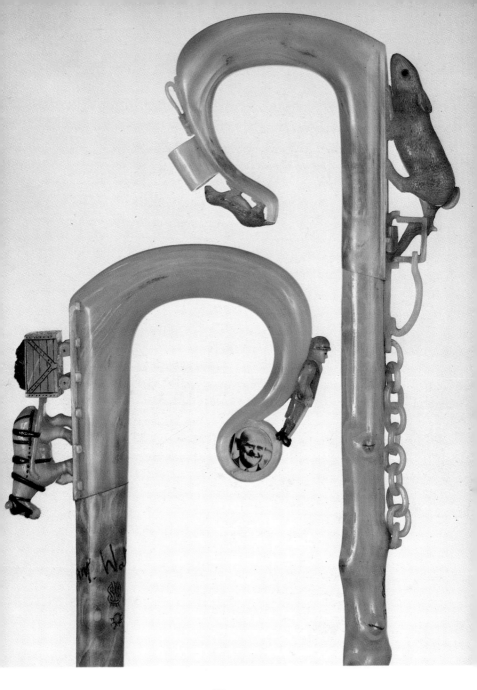

**Plate 5.**
*(a) The pit pony. (b) The gin trap.*

**Plate 6.**
*(a) Double carting. (b) The Gipsy caravan.*

38

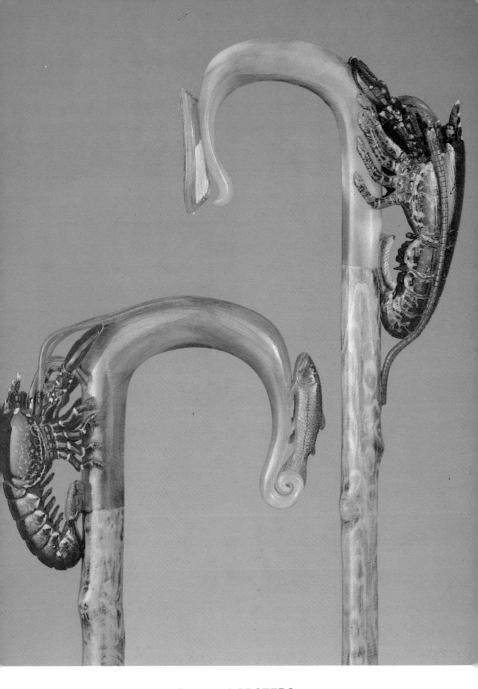

**Plate 7. LOBSTERS**

*(a) Male. (b) Female.*

**Plate 8.**
*Golden Plover
(suspended by reef knot)*

# THE COCK PHEASANT'S HEAD
*Plate 4 (b)*
*Drawing page 42*

After one becomes really expert in the art of stick dressing it is sometimes possible to come across a ram's horn that will allow you to shank it from the nose end, in other words the opposite way round. The benefit of being able to do this is that one is able to carve the pheasant's beak without exposing any of the pith that runs through every horn. This is beneficial when the stick dresser wants to carve any bird's head; however it is seldom one comes across a horn that will allow one to do this.

Before any carving is attempted it is advisable first to obtain a good old cock pheasant's head that has plenty of character. I must point out that we have a very mixed breed of pheasants today so it is not every head that is suitable. Having selected a suitable specimen it is very easy to keep it in a suitable condition by placing the pheasant's head in a deep freezer, and this goes for any other bird, fish or small animal that one wants to hang onto. If a suitable horn has been selected it is possible to carve a life-sized head. In order to do this it is necessary to take one's measurements with a set of calipers, and by doing this it is possible to work to a very fine degree of

*Raw horn.*

# THE COCK PHEASANT'S HEAD

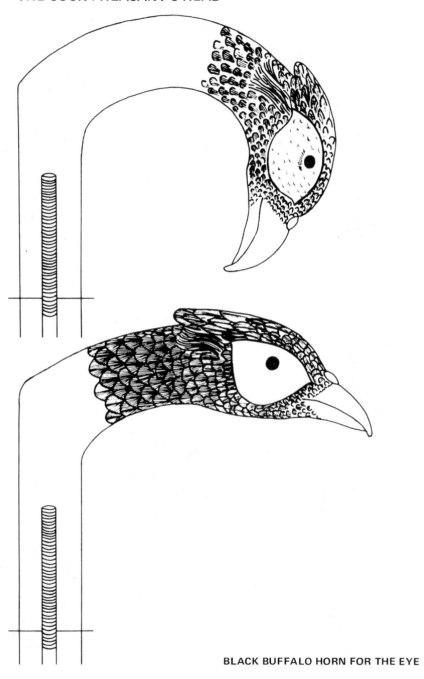

**BLACK BUFFALO HORN FOR THE EYE**

42

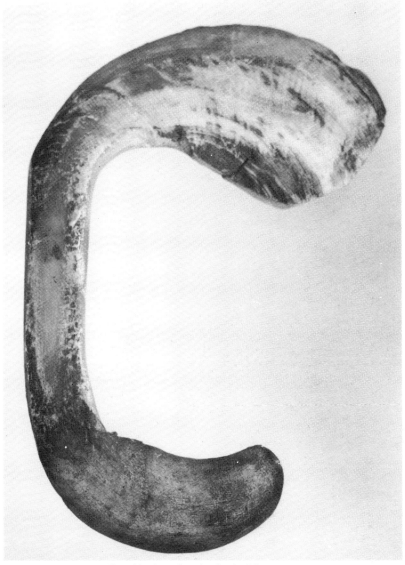

*Roughly shaped, to be shanked from nose.*

perfection. Particular attention must be paid to the feathering of the head and the small feathers up against the bird's beak and how they gradually get larger and change shape as they go over the head and down the neck. Also note how different the feathers are that cover the ear holes on the bird's head. In one's carvings it is difficult to get character and capture the lifelike alertness of the bird. I always find my carvings are dead until I put the eyes

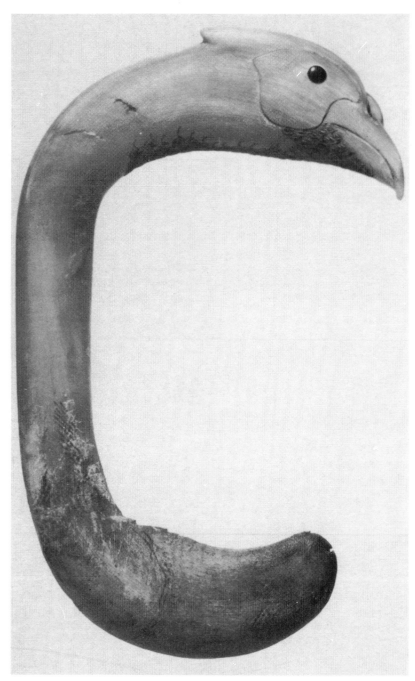

*Shaped and eyes fitted.*

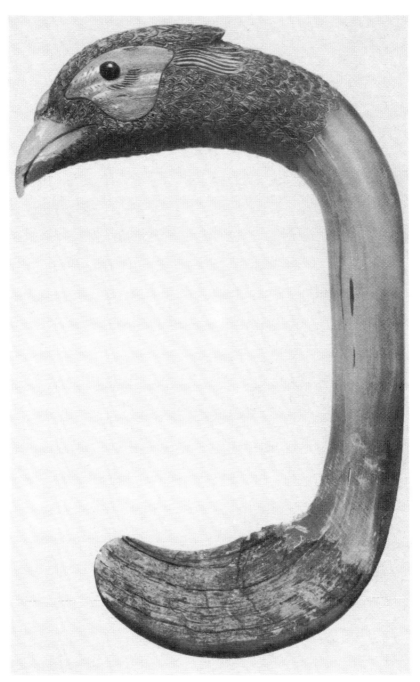

*Feathered, ready for colouring and shanking.*

*Details of feathering.*

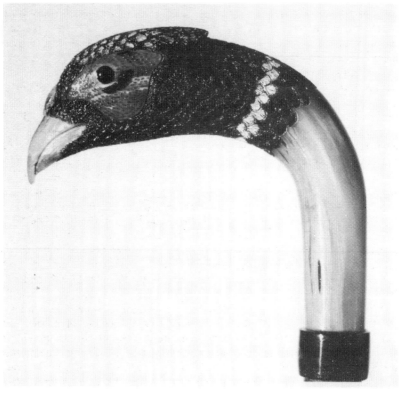

*Finished.*

46

in, and if one can only get these eyes just right it makes all the difference in the world. The carving of the feathers can be done with either a very fine chisel, or an electric soldering iron taking great care not to slip, so it is advisable to anchor one's hand in a firm position. Here again, as with the trout, the colouring is done entirely with ink. After a while one becomes very confident about using ink as a colouring material, as it has the great advantage of not hiding the natural texture and grain of the horn. This particular walking stick is a great favourite with those who enjoy shooting as a pastime, but as for myself I prefer to see the old cock pheasant wandering around my farm. What sight is nicer than to observe the old cock sunning himself when his plumage is at its best about February or March. One would think that these old birds knew exactly when the shooting season is over, they become so much tamer as the Spring rolls nearer. It will take about 60 or 70 hours to make a thoroughly good pheasant's head that would do the bird justice.

## THE GIN TRAP
*Plate 5 (b)*

This particular stick leaves me with the most vivid memories because my brothers and I never used to get any wages or pocket money. The gin trap, a quantity of snares, the long net and a few ferrets, these were our source of income. This was the only life we knew, so what we never had we never missed. Our parents provided the food and the clothing. By the age of 10 I became expert at setting gin traps and snaring rabbits. I never did care much about the ferrets. Some of them were quiet to handle while others would fasten their teeth in your fingers. Sometimes they would grab your chin if you were a bit careless and got too near to them with your face. One day my elder brother and a friend were ferreting a rabbit hole when the ferret came out covered in blood. They thought that this was a bit strange so they started to dig and the first thing they came across was the brush of a fox. This fox was in such a small hole that it had to be dragged out still alive, but out of this same hole came seven weasels. Whatever could be the explanation for this? Is it possible that these weasels had been hunting the fox? The ferret never recovered from its ordeal! The other day I asked my brother, who is a farmer like myself, if he could recall this incident and he remembered the affair very well and could take me to the place it happened even today. We live only about five miles apart and are both tenants of the Duke of Northumberland. Today the gin trap is not allowed to be used, which may be just as well because it was undoubtedly a cruel thing. However there were so many rabbits in those days that you simply caught them by whatever means you could. On the nose of this particular stick I have carved the tunnel trap. It was by this method that the gamekeepers caught the weasels. The method used was to take a field drainpipe and place it at the foot of a wall or on a hedge back or in some other suitable place where the keepers knew there would be a weasel or a stoat about. The drainpipe would be covered over with

47

a few loose stones leaving the ends open, and the trap would be set in place. It did not matter at which open end of the drainpipe the trap would be set, for the weasel or stoat is such an inquisitive creature that it simply has to investigate this new hole as it was not there yesterday. Inevitably this leads to its death. What an expert killer of a rabbit this creature is. The usual method would be to enter a rabbit warren and bolt its victim out into the open field. Then it would begin to circle its prey getting a little nearer every time until it was within striking distance. The target was a large vein behind the rabbit's ear from which it would suck the blood. To avoid the kicking feet of the rabbit, the weasel would keep hold of the vein and at the same time lie over the back of the victim out of harm's way.

In those days we had the local "carrier" who used to call once a week and take away the rabbits. Also he bought the spare eggs and butter from the farmer's wife and in return he had a supply of provisions for the household. He always carried paraffin for, as we had no electricity, our lighting was all paraffin lamps. A couple of rabbits had to weigh not less than 5 lbs during the winter but a good couple of rabbits could weigh more than 5 lbs. However, during the summer, it could take perhaps six or more young rabbits to reach this weight. We got about 3p a couple during the summer and about 6p a couple during November, December and January.

## THE PIT PONY
### *Plate 5 (a)*

In carving some of my fancy sticks I have tried to portray the passage of time. So it came about that my thoughts wandered to the small pit pony. Pits like Ashington used to work with a fairly big pony, while others used the very small Shetland pony that was about 40" high. Their fodder went down to them and they had their stables underground. Special care had to be taken about the type of harness they used to wear; for instance, the pony's head and eyes had to be protected from falling rocks. The collar and the rest of the harness along the pony's back had to be designed so that they would not catch on the seam roof under which the pony worked.

On the nose end of the head I have carved the pit deputy as I remember him as a boy when visiting my grandmother who lived in a mining village at Prudhoe. The main road went past grandmother's door. Beyond the road was a line of very poor garden fencing made of slabs of wood. Sitting on their "hunkers" would be a number of pitmen playing pitch and toss. I never could understand at the time how they could stay in this position for such a long time. As the pitman nearly always had a greyhound or whippet there would also be a number of these dogs across the road. As a small farm boy not yet at school I used to sit on grandmother's doorstep and watch this scene. One man I can clearly recall was an ex-pitman with a wooden leg. He was always arguing with the group of men who were playing pitch and toss. I realise now that I was watching a union man at work. This would be about 1918–1919, certainly before 1920 because I hadn't then been to school. Another sight I never could get over at this time was this: if a horse should leave its droppings on the road outside anyone's door that person would take a shovel and a pail, gather up the droppings and then take them to his garden. I realise now how important it was for them to do this but at the time I thought they were mad. Grandmother used to tell many stories about the pits and pitmen. For instance, if a pitman forgot anything on his way to work he wouldn't go to work that day as it was a sign of bad luck and if he met a woman on his way to work in the early hours of the morning this was taken as another sign of bad luck. The story she used to tell about the rats leaving one colliery to go to another used to fascinate me. These rats must have been like an army on the move. They would travel along a cart track or even a footpath, so many abreast and always at night. If a pitman was going to the early shift in the early hours of the morning it must have been a hair-raising experience meeting this quantity of rats on the move. It was taken as another sign of bad luck for the rats to leave a pit. Was it another case of rats leaving a sinking ship? After I had finished this stick I got the late Sam Watson to autograph it for me. Sam at the time of making the stick was the Durham miners leader.

It took about 200 hours to make. (Dorset horn used.)

## THE GIPSY CARAVAN
*Plate 6 (b)*

Today we no longer have with us the old fashioned type of gipsy. Around the countryside there are many places that were favoured camping sites including the quiet country lane. It was just such a place that we had on the boundary between us and our neighbouring farmer. As a boy the ponies and young lurcher dogs used to claim my main attention. When the puppies became strong enough to travel they would be tied to the axle of one of the back wheels. In time they became so used to travelling in this manner that as older dogs they automatically took up this position when on the move.

The young ponies were my favourites. It used to be amusing to watch a young pony to go to the side of the road, grab a few mouthfulls of grass, then set off trotting to catch up with the caravan. It would repeat this performance over and over again. I often wondered why the gipsy man whilst walking beside the caravan used to strike the brush undergrowth on the road verge with a light piece of stick. The answer to this was given to me some twenty-years later. A one armed fisherman from a local fishing village had a horse and flat cart which he used for going round the district selling fish. One day when I was ploughing beside the road I saw the fisherman doing exactly this very thing. Every few yards he would strike the undergrowth so I asked him why he did this. He only made one brief remark. "Pheasant's nests." So after many years this gipsy problem was solved by a fisherman. Country people and the gipsies got on very well together; there was always a "live and let live" realtionship. Everyone knew what the lurcher dogs were for, that the menfolk would poach at night and that if some of the landlord's game found its way into their poaching pockets, the best of luck to them. As for poaching

I watched salmon being taken before I was two-years-old and by the time I was eight I actually took part in salmon poaching expeditions myself. Almost everyone living in the upper reaches of the North Tyne helped themselves to these salmon for we didn't think we were doing anything wrong. Nature had provided a source of food and as there were thousands of salmon in these waters it was up to everyone to make the most of this bonanza. In any case there was hardly any likelihood of being caught. A story used to be told about the two policemen who met on a bridge over a stream. As they stood talking they both observed a salmon in the water below the bridge, but neither let on to the other that he had seen this fish. So time came for them each to go his own way. A little while after they both turned back with the result that they again met on the middle of the bridge. They decided to halve the fish.

Our farm house and buildings were situated about 400 yards from the banks of the North Tyne. When the river was in flood the water came right up to the garden gate and an area of our land flooded up to about 20 acres. After the flood water had subsided a small lake of about a quarter of an acre in size remained. On one occasion there were so many salmon left stranded in this small lake that we had to lead them home with a horse and cart. On another occasion when there was a cloudburst on the fells above Keilder, peat moss was brought down with the flood water. The water was so impregnated with the moss that it choked all the salmon in that part of the river. On my way to school I went past hundreds of these beautiful fish lying dead in the fields where the flood water had left them. All of them had their gills choked tightly with peat moss. The strangest sight I ever observed was a dead blackfaced ewe floating down the middle of the flood water with a live rabbit sitting on its body.

## DOUBLE CARTING

*Plate 6 (a)*

Before the Second World War it was the custom in Northumberland and along the Scottish Borders for one horseman to work with two horses and two carts. On the tillage farms there would always be a number of women workers. They were called "bondagers" but why I do not know. These women would help to fill the carts and do other duties on the farm such as feeding cattle during the winter and placing the sheaves so that the man stacking the corn hadn't to reach too far for each sheaf. If a stacker had to reach for his sheaves, the stack he was building was always very difficult to keep right, I know because I have done it. What happened was that the man on the cart loaded with about 100 to 140 sheaves of corn would fork each one singly from the cart to the "bondager". He would flip the sheaf in midair so that it would land beside the feet of the "bondager" who would always be standing in the middle of the stack. In turn she would place the sheaf just beside the  knee of the stacker who had to only reach a few inches to place each sheaf in position. The stacker worked in a kneeling position all day and, in order to protect his knees, would make himself knee-pads or simply get his wife to sew extra cloth on the knees of his trousers. The latter method was the better of the two.

Can I describe to you what was the order of the day for a horseman when I first started work in 1928? The horses had to be fed and mucked out at 5.30 a.m. Then you went into the house and had a bit of breakfast. At 6.15 a.m. you would be back in the stable to "curry-comb" and brush your horses, not forgetting to remove any further droppings. The farm steward walked into the stable at 6.25 a.m. strolled round the stable looking for faults and at 6.28 a.m. we were given our orders for the day. We had to harness up and move out for starting time at 6.30 a.m. on the dot and it did not matter whether it was winter or summer. It could be still so dark that you yoked your horses by feel. After the steward had given the first horseman his orders he then continued down the line through the lower ranks of horsemen until he reached the "odd laddie". Another term for the "odd laddie" was to call him the "turnip dick". What a life the "turnip dick" had! He had to do all the odd jobs about the farm. For instance, if you had managed to get 10 loads of turnips in yesterday and could only manage nine today there had to be an enquiry. My other two brothers and I were the farmer's sons but that made no difference. You had to do as the steward said. In the mornings we worked till 11.45 a.m., started up again at 1.15 p.m. and worked till 6 p.m., winter and summer, daylight or dark. We started work in this regimented manner and finished work in the same order. I was eventually promoted to drive the two in-foal mares. They would have to work every day right up to the time of foaling. One could always estimate just how long it was safe to continue working them. A wax-like substance started ousing out of the mare's teats about three weeks before it was due to foal. This gradually got longer until it dropped off. The mare had now to stop working because it was getting quite near to foaling time, perhaps another day or two at the latest. In spite of working with these in-foal mares, I was only once ever on the spot at the right time to see a foal actually being born. If everything is just as it should be, the birth is all over in a matter of seconds, and the foal could be on its feet within half-an-hour. To me a young foal is still the most lovely of all the four-legged creatures.

How we longed for the spring to come so that we could get the work horses out on to the grass. It made no difference to starting time or the hours of work, but it did make a lot of difference on Sundays because we could lie in bed for as long as we liked during the morning. There was only one fly in the ointment. When it was your turn to milk the farmhouse cows—about two or three of them—the custom was to get up about 6.30 a.m., get the cows in and milk them, then back to bed for the rest of the morning.

The horn used for "Double Carting" was from a trophy head. It was inscribed "Dali! Shot in Alaska 1902." This took approximately 300 hours to make. On the nose end is carved a bit strap buckle.

## THE LOBSTER MALE AND FEMALE
### *Plate 7*
As my farm is only three miles from the fishing villages of Craster and

Boulmer I have several friends among the fishermen, with the result that the Boulmer fishermen challenged me to carve a lobster in a ram's horn on a walking stick head and one Sunday morning Ray Stanton presented me with a male lobster. There is a considerable difference between the male and female; I will point out the main difference as far as carving is concerned later on. The only way for me to preserve the lobster was to put it in a container and place it in the deep-freeze. This lobster was given to me at the start of the season which begins in the Autumn. Time after time I would take out the lobster to have another look at him, with the result that I would be looking after the farm stock and doing other work, but my mind would be on this lobster, wondering and planning how to approach the carving. This went on for several months. During that time Ray would have a dig at me and ask how I was getting on with the lobster.

As it had taken me three years to solve the carving of another head, I had no intention of panicking over the lobster! Then, one day the whole operation solved itself. The main problem had been that I had been looking at the *whole* lobster. What I had to do was break it down into various stages; get them in their proper order for carving, and do one stage at a time. Again the programme was to draw a scaled down model of the lobster, so that it could be carved from the very small amount of horn that was available. In order to balance the horn head, the problem is always to find a suitable subject for the nose end; in this case I chose to carve the Grilse. The main difference in the female lobster was that the shell covering the lobster's body and also the tail was very much larger than the male. The fishermen said the reason for this was protection first to the eggs that are attached to the female's body, then to the young after they hatch out. What the fishermen do not understand is that the authorities allow these female lobsters to be caught and sold when bearing eggs.

As a farmer it is astounding to me that breeding stock is allowed to be plundered in this way; it is like a farmer slaughtering his in-lamb ewes a few weeks before lambing. Both in farming and, it would appear, in fishing there are some strange decisions made by people in high authority. I sincerely hope that the female lobster will once again become a protected creature.

## THE REEF KNOT INSPIRATION
*Plate 8*

Some years ago I decided to leave my farm in Northumberland to attend the cattle sales in the Hereford district, the centre of the cattle sales. I booked into a hotel not far from the cathedral. As there was plenty of time to spare between breakfast and the start of the sale, I decided to stroll down the street towards the cathedral and it was a stroll that was to change the whole future of my "hobby". I entered a small bookshop that sold various other items and on looking around I observed they had a lending library on the second floor, so up the stairs I went. Half-way up the stairs on a small landing there was a glass case with a wood carving inside; I was simply dumbfounded at what I saw. I wonder how many other people have had the pleasure of looking at this wonderful piece of work.

The wood carving was done by Thomas Wilkinson Wallis in 1863 and had taken him a whole year to carve and went on to win the World Exhibition in 1864.

The theme was a woodcock hanging by its legs with a length of string from a rotten outhouse door, the string and the reef knot were carved in wood. There was, of course, an awful lot more carving associated with this masterpiece.

After returning home I would wonder how could I possibly make use of the reef knot and at the same time hang various game birds up by the neck in a dead position. Eventually I worked out the design to which I have since worked.

From the drawing on a horn of the position of a Golden Plover it is possible to see how one is able to do so. Now it is only possible to do this with an extremely large horn such as a Dorset horn or a Wiltshire; and one has to have patience and a fair ability to draw the finished head to a fraction of an inch before any work is done on the horn. I have finally got the work down to about 250 hours after many years of experience. It took me all winter with my first one. I now use the reef knot as my special insignia on the shanks of all the sticks I make.

In writing this book I have described in detail just one of the many crafts that were practised in the rural part of north Northumberland. One can hardly realise that in the space of one lifetime many of our country crafts have completely disappeared along with the generation that practised them.

I hope that I have given enough information to encourage people in other parts of the world to take up this very rewarding pastime of turning a knarled old ram's horn into a thing of lasting beauty.

# ROMAN WALL BOOKS

## HADRIAN'S WALL RECONSTRUCTED
Magnificent paintings in full colour showing the Roman Wall
as it was when built.
*Paintings by R. Embleton. Text by C. M. Daniels.*
£2.00

## A SHORT GUIDE TO THE ROMAN WALL
*by T. H. Rowland*
£1.20

## HOUSESTEADS IN THE DAYS OF THE ROMANS
*by Ronald Embleton*
90p

## ROMAN COOK BOOK
80p